A LIFEGUIDE BIBLE STUDY

PSALMS
Prayers of the Heart

*12 Studies
for individuals or groups*

Eugene H. Peterson

With Notes for Leaders

INTERVARSITY PRESS
DOWNERS GROVE, ILLINOIS 60515

InterVarsity Press is the book-publishing division of InterVarsity Christian Fellowship, a student movement active on campus at hundreds of universities, colleges and schools of nursing. For information about local and regional activities, write Public Relations Dept., InterVarsity Christian Fellowship, 6400 Schroeder Rd., P.O. Box 7895, Madison, WI 53707-7895.

Distributed in Canada through InterVarsity Press, 860 Denison St., Unit 3, Markham, Ontario L3R 4H1, Canada.

All Scripture quotations, unless otherwise indicated, are taken from the Holy Bible, New International Version. Copyright © 1973, 1978, International Bible Society. Used by permission of Zondervan Bible Publishers.

Cover photograph: Robert McKendrick

ISBN 0-8308-1034-X

Printed in the United States of America

18	17	16	15	14	13	12	11	10	9	8	7	6	5	4	3	2
99	98	97	96	95	94	93	92	91	90	89	88					

Contents

105982

Getting the Most
from LifeGuide Bible Studies

Many of us long to fill our minds and our lives with Scripture. We desire to be transformed by its message. LifeGuide Bible Studies are designed to be an exciting and challenging way to do just that. They help us to be guided by God's Word in every area of life.

How They Work

LifeGuides have a number of distinctive features. Perhaps the most important is that they are *inductive* rather than *deductive*. In other words, they lead us to *discover* what the Bible says rather than simply *telling* us what it says.

They are also thought provoking. They help us to think about the meaning of the passage so that we can truly understand what the author is saying. The questions require more than one-word answers.

The studies are personal. Questions expose us to the promises, assurances, exhortations and challenges of God's Word. They are designed to allow the Scriptures to renew our minds so that we can be transformed by the Spirit of God. This is the ultimate goal of all Bible study.

The studies are versatile. They are designed for student, neighborhood and church groups. They are also effective for individual study.

How They're Put Together

LifeGuides also have a distinctive format. Each study need take no more than forty-five minutes in a group setting or thirty minutes in personal study—unless you choose to take more time.

The studies can be used within a quarter system in a church and fit well in a semester or trimester system on a college campus. If a guide has more than thirteen studies, it is divided into two or occasionally three parts of approximately twelve studies each.

LifeGuides use a workbook format. Space is provided for writing answers to each question. This is ideal for personal study and allows group members to prepare in advance for the discussion.

The studies also contain leader's notes. They show how to lead a group discussion, provide additional background information on certain questions, give helpful tips on group dynamics and suggest ways to deal with problems which may arise during the discussion. With such helps, someone with little or no experience can lead an effective study.

Suggestions for Individual Study

1. As you begin each study, pray that God will help you to understand and apply the passage to your life.

2. Read and reread the assigned Bible passage to familiarize yourself with what the author is saying. In the case of book studies, you may want to read through the entire book prior to the first study. This will give you a helpful overview of its contents.

3. A good modern translation of the Bible, rather than the King James Version or a paraphrase, will give you the most help. The New International Version, the New American Standard Bible and the Revised Standard Version are all recommended. However, the questions in this guide are based on the New International Version.

4. Write your answers in the space provided in the study guide. This will help you to express your understanding of the passage clearly.

5. It might be good to have a Bible dictionary handy. Use it to look up any unfamiliar words, names or places.

Suggestions for Group Study

1. Come to the study prepared. Follow the suggestions for individual study mentioned above. You will find that careful preparation will greatly enrich your time spent in group discussion.

2. Be willing to participate in the discussion. The leader of your group will not be lecturing. Instead, he or she will be encouraging the members of the group to discuss what they have learned from the passage. The leader will be asking the questions that are found in this guide. Plan to share what God has taught you in your individual study.

3. Stick to the passage being studied. Your answers should be based on the verses which are the focus of the discussion and not on outside authorities such as commentaries or speakers. This guide deliberately avoids jumping from book to book or passage to passage. Each study focuses on only one passage. Book studies are generally designed to lead you through the book in the order in which it was written. This will help you follow the author's argument.

4. Be sensitive to the other members of the group. Listen attentively when they share what they have learned. You may be surprised by their insights! Link what you say to the comments of others so the group stays on the topic. Also, be affirming whenever you can. This will encourage some of the more hesitant members of the group to participate.

5. Be careful not to dominate the discussion. We are sometimes so eager to share what we have learned that we leave too little opportunity for others to respond. By all means participate! But allow others to also.

6. Expect God to teach you through the passage being discussed and through the other members of the group. Pray that you will have an enjoyable and profitable time together.

7. If you are the discussion leader, you will find additional suggestions and helpful ideas for each study in the leader's notes. These are found at the back of the guide.

Introducing Psalms

People look into mirrors to see how they look; they look into the Psalms to find out who they are. A mirror is an excellent way to learn about our appearance; the Psalms are the biblical way to discover ourselves. With a mirror we detect a new wrinkle here, an old wart there. We use a mirror when shaving or applying make-up to improve, if we can, the face we present to the world. With the Psalms we bring into awareness an ancient sorrow, release a latent joy. We use the Psalms to present ourselves before God as honestly and thoroughly as we are able. A mirror shows us the shape of our nose and the curve of our chin, things we otherwise know only through the reports of others. The Psalms show us the shape of our souls and the curve of our sin, realities deep within us, hidden and obscured, for which we need focus and names.

The Psalms are poetry and the Psalms are prayer. These two features, the poetry and the prayer, need to be kept in mind always. If either is forgotten the Psalms will not only be misunderstood but misused.

Poetry is language used with intensity. It is not, as so many suppose, decorative speech. Poets tell us what our eyes, blurred with too much gawking, and our ears, dulled with too much chatter, miss around and within us. Poets use words to drag us into the depths of reality itself, not by reporting on how life is, but by pushing-pulling us into the middle of it. Poetry gets at the heart of existence. Far from being cosmetic language, it is intestinal. It is root language. Poetry doesn't so much tell us something we never knew as bring into recognition what was latent or forgotten or overlooked. The Psalms are almost entirely this kind of language. Knowing this, we will not be looking primarily for ideas about God in the Psalms or for direction in moral conduct. We will expect, rather, to find exposed and sharpened what it means to be human beings before God.

Prayer is language used in relation to God. It gives utterance to what we sense or want or respond to before God. God speaks to us; our answers are our prayers. The answers are not always articulate. Silence, sighs, groaning—these also constitute responses. But always God is involved, whether in darkness or light, whether in faith or despair. This is hard to get used to. Our habit is to talk *about* God, not *to* him. We love discussing God. But the Psalms resist such discussions. They are provided not to teach us about God but to train us in responding to him. We don't learn the Psalms until we are praying them.

Those two features, the poetry and the prayer, account for both the excitement and the difficulty in studying the Psalms. The *poetry* requires that we deal with our actual humanity—these words dive beneath the surfaces of pose and pretense straight into the depths. We are more comfortable with prose, the laid-back language of our ordinary discourse. The *prayer* requires that we deal with God—this God who is determined on nothing less than the total renovation of our lives. We would rather have a religious bull session.

One editorial feature of the Psalms helps to keep these distinctive qualities of the Psalms before us. The Psalms are arranged into five books. At the end of Psalms 41, 72, 89, 106 and 150 formula sentences indicate a conclusion. Because of these miniconclusions the Psalms are usually printed (in English translations) as Book I (Psalms 1—41), Book II (42—72), Book III (73—89), Book IV (90—106) and Book V (107—150).

This five-book arrangement matches the five-book beginning of the Bible, deeply embedded in our minds as the five books of Moses. The five books of Moses are matched by the five books of David like two five-fingered hands clasping one another in greeting. In the five books of Moses God addresses us by his word, calling us into being and shaping our salvation. In the five books of David we personally re-spond to this personal word that addresses us. Prayer is answering speech. Every word that God speaks to us must be answered by us. God's word has not done its complete work until it evokes an answer from us. All our answers are prayers. The Psalms train us in this an-swering speech, this language that responds to all God's creating and saving words targeted to our lives.

It is important to notice this well, for it shifts our interpretive stance. Our usual approach to God's word is to ask, What is God saying to me? That is almost always the correct question when reading Scripture. But in the Psalms the question is, How do I answer the God who speaks to me? In the Psalms we do not primarily learn what God *says* to us, but how to honestly, devoutly and faithfully *answer* his words to us. In the course of acquiring language we learn how to answer our par-ents, our teachers, our employers and our friends, but we do not get very much practice in answering God. The Psalms train us in answering God. And so we bring a somewhat different mindset to the Psalms than we do to the rest of Scripture—we are learning to *pray* not study, although the two activities will always be interconnected.

We know almost nothing of the circumstances in which the 150 Psalms were written. David is the most named author, but most are anonymous. But that hardly matters, for the life-settings of the Psalms are not geographical or cultural but *interior.* Calvin called them "an anatomy of all the parts of the soul." Everything that anyone can feel or experience in relation to God is in these prayers. You will find them the best place in Scripture to explore all the parts of your life and then to say who you are and what is in you—guilt, anger, salvation, praise— to the God who loves, judges and saves you in Jesus Christ. These twelve studies are designed to guide you into twelve interior dimen-sions of your life and bring them to expression before God.

1
Praying Our Inattention

Psalm 1

Psalm 1 is not prayer, exactly, but the preface to prayer. We do not begin to pray by praying, but by coming to attention. Psalm 1 is the biblical preparation for a life of prayer. Step by step it detaches us from activities and words that distract us from God so that we can be attentive before him. Most of us can't step immediately from the noisy high-stimulus world into the quiet concentration of prayer. We need a way of transition. Psalm 1 provides a kind of entryway into the place of prayer.

1. Do you feel a gap (or chasm!) between "real life" (work, school, family) and your prayer life? Explain.

2. Read Psalm 1. What contrasts do you notice in the psalm?

3. The first word in the psalm is *blessed.* (Some translate it *happy.*) What kind of expectations should that bring to our life of prayer?

4. What significance do you see in the progression from *walk* to *stand* to *sit* (v. 1)?

5. "The law of the LORD" is contrasted with the words *counsel, way* and *seat.* What does this contrast bring out?

6. The psalmist describes the person who *delights* in God's law (v. 2). What is your emotional response to Scripture—not what you *believe* about it but how you *feel* about it?

7. *Tree* is the central metaphor of the psalm (v. 3). Put your imagination to use. How are law-delighting people like trees?

8. In what ways are the wicked like chaff (vv. 4-6)?

9. How do these two radically different portraits (the tree-righteous and the chaff-wicked) motivate you to delight in God's Word?

10. How does meditation—listening to God speak to us through Scripture—prepare us for prayer?

How can you install a procedure for meditation in your life?

11. Some prayer is spontaneous—a word of thanks, a cry of pain. Other prayer is routine—at meals, in public worship. But a *life* of prayer requires preparation, a procedure for moving from inattention to attention. The same procedure will not suit everyone. How can you develop a procedure that fits your circumstances and development?

2
Praying Our Intimidation

Psalm 2

We wake up each day in a world noisy with boasting, violent with guns, arrogant with money. How can we avoid being intimidated? What use can prayer have in the face of governments and armies and millionaires? None, if God is not at work; all, if God is. Psalm 2, like Psalm 1, is pre-prayer—an act of orientation that prepares us to pray. The orientation this time is not personal but political. Psalm 2 prepares us to pray in political as well as personal dimensions. God is as much at work in the public sphere as he is in the personal, and our prayers are as needful there as in our personal lives.

1. Do you feel as responsible to pray for the nation, society and culture as you do for self, friends and church? Explain.

2. Read Psalm 2. Compare the opening nouns and verbs in Psalm 1:1-3 with those in Psalm 2:1-3. What differences in orientation do they suggest between these two psalms?

3. Compare the first verse of Psalm 1 to the last in Psalm 2. What do we learn from these two *blesseds?*

---

4. *Meditates* in Psalm 1:2 and *plot* in Psalm 2:1 are the same word in Hebrew. How is the word used differently in the two passages?

---

5. How does the Lord view the vaunted power of nations (vv. 4-6)?

Do you maintain this perspective of light humor when you watch the evening news on television? Explain.

---

6. "Anointed One" in verse 2 is *Messiah* in Hebrew, *Christ* in Greek. What in this psalm reminds you of Jesus?

---

7. It has been traditional for Christians to pray this psalm on Easter Day. What in the psalm especially suits it for this occasion?

8. The psalm begins and ends with references to kings and rulers (vv. 2-3, 10-12). How do they relate to the King enthroned by the Lord (v. 6)?

What impact does this have on the way we pray?

9. It is always easier to pray for personal needs than political situations. But Psalm 2 is entirely political. Knowing this, what responsibility do we have as American citizens living in Christ's kingdom?

10. Name three rulers (presidents, kings, prime ministers or dictators). Pray for them faithfully this week.

3
Praying
Our Trouble
Psalm 3

P salm 3 is the first prayer in the Psalter. Psalms 1 and 2 prepared us for prayer; Psalm 3 prays. Prayer begins in a realization that we cannot help ourselves, so we must reach out to God. "Help!" is the basic prayer. We are in trouble, deep trouble. If God cannot get us out, we are lost; if God can get us out, we are saved. If we don't know that we need help, prayer will always be peripheral to our lives, a matter of mood and good manners. But the moment we know we are in trouble, prayer is a life-or-death matter.

1. What is the worst trouble you were in this last week? Where did you go for help? Did you get help?

2. Read Psalm 3. This psalm was written when David fled from his son Absalom. Briefly summarize this story from 2 Samuel 15—18.

3. *Deliver/deliverance* is a key word in this psalm. What do we learn about the nature of deliverance through its various uses here?

4. David's prayer naturally divides into five sections: verses 1-2, 3-4, 5-6, 7 and 8. Name each stanza with a single word or phrase.

What progression do you see from each section to the next?

5. David describes his foes in verses 1-2. Do you ever feel overwhelmed by threatening people or circumstances? Give an example.

6. What actions is God described as taking in this psalm?

Are you used to thinking of God in these ways? Explain.

7. What actions is David described as taking in the psalm?

To what extent do these characterize you when trouble arises?

8. The emotional center of the psalm is verse 5. Take this seriously and ponder its significance. When we are sleeping, what are we doing? What is God doing?

9. What kind of trouble are you in right now?

10. What in this psalm do you think will help you to pray your trouble?

11. Take an image or phrase from Psalm 3 and use it to pray your trouble. Plan to continue through the week.

4
Praying Our Creation

Psalm 8

Prayer is an orienting act. We begin to discover *who* we are when we realize *where* we are. Disorientation is a terrible experience. If we cannot locate our place, we are in confusion and anxiety. We are also in danger, for we are apt to act inappropriately. If we are among enemies and don't know it, we may lose our life. If we are among friends and don't know it, we may miss good relationships. If we are alongside a cliff and don't know it, we may lose our footing. While praying Psalm 8, we find out where we are and some important aspects of who we are.

---

1. When traveling, have you ever awakened and not known where you were? The bed is unfamiliar; the room is strange; you look out the window and don't recognize anything. What does it feel like to be disoriented?

---

2. Read Psalm 8. Note the first and last sentences. What is the significance of these bracketing sentences for the psalm even before we know its contents?

3. Why do you think the psalmist contrasts what children and infants say with what foes and avengers say in verse 2?

4. Browse through the psalm and note every word that refers to what God has created. How do these things reveal God's glory?

5. Bernard Lonergan once said that when an animal doesn't have anything to do it goes to sleep; when humans don't have anything to do they ask questions. What kind of question do we find at almost the exact center of this psalm (v. 4)?

What kind of answer is adequate to it?

6. What evidence do we have that God is mindful of us, that he cares for us?

7. Verse 5 comments on our *position* in creation. How does it contrast with positions we are put in by nonbiblical authorities?

8. Verse 6 comments on our *responsibility* over creation. In what ways do you feel or not feel responsibility for your environment?

9. The psalm lists six creatures (vv. 7-8) over which we have God-entrusted responsibility. Name six other items over which you accept responsibility.

10. "Ruler" and "under his feet" (v. 6) can be twisted into excuses to exploit and pillage. What is there in this psalm to prevent such twisting?

11. How does Psalm 8 compare with the way you view yourself?

12. What adjustments do you need to make to view yourself as God views you?

13. Some people think of themselves as "a little higher than the heavenly beings"; others think "a little lower than the beasts of the field." In what area has Psalm 8 corrected your self-image?

14. The psalmist concludes, as he began, with praise. Pray, praising God and using this psalm as the basis for your praise.

5
Praying
Our Sin

Psalm 51

Alongside the basic fact that God made us good (Ps 8) is the equally basic fact that we have gone wrong. We pray our sins to get to the truth about ourselves and to find out how God treats sinners. Our experience of sin does not consist in doing some bad things but in *being* bad. It is a fundamental condition of our existence, not a temporary lapse into error. Praying our sin isn't resolving not to sin anymore; it is discovering what God has resolved to do with us as sinners.

1. As Christians, we know we are sinful. Why then is it so painful to be confronted with a specific sin?

2. Read Psalm 51. The psalm title refers this prayer to David's adultery with Bathsheba. Briefly summarize the details of this episode in 2 Samuel 11—12.

3. How many different synonyms for sin are in his prayer?

What does this tell us about the nature of sin?

_____

4. What is God asked to do about sin? (Count and name the verbs.)

_____

5. If I have been a sinner from birth (v. 5), sin must be something more than doing wrong things. What else could it be?

_____

6. Verses 1-9 exhibit a heightened awareness of sin. What do they make you aware of?

_____

7. Verse 10 is the center sentence. How does it center the prayer?

What parallel does _create_ have with Genesis 1:1?

8. Forgiveness is an internal action with external consequences. What are some of them (vv. 13-17)?

9. What do you understand a "broken and contrite heart" to be (v. 17)?

What is your experience of this condition?

10. According to verses 18-19, what is the relationship between personal forgiveness and social righteousness?

11. Psalm 51 makes us aware of how sinful we are, and it makes us less actively sinful. How do you see it working that way in you?

12. Be quiet before God. In silence confess your sins to him. Accept his forgiveness and grace.

6
Praying Our Salvation

Psalm 103

W hat God has done for us far exceeds anything we have done for or against him. The summary word for this excessive, undeserved, unexpected act by God is *salvation*. Prayer explores the country of salvation, tramping the contours, smelling the flowers, touching the outcroppings. There is more to do than recognize the sheer fact of salvation and witness to it; there are unnumbered details of grace, of mercy, of blessing to be appreciated and savored. Prayer is the means by which we do this.

---

1. Think of one of the best things that ever happened to you. Describe some of the details of why it was so good.

---

2. Read Psalm 103. This psalm expresses the *experience* (not the doctrine) of salvation. This is what it *feels* like to be saved. What are your general impressions of the psalm?

3. Note the first and last sentences. How does this bracketing affect your understanding of the psalm's contents?

4. Salvation is more richly complex than we sometimes think. What five actions of God add up to salvation (vv. 3-5)?

Which of these have you benefited from?

5. How did God make his ways known to Moses and Israel (v. 7)?

6. What astounding statements about God does the psalmist make in verses 8-14?

Which ones in particular expand what is puny in your thinking?

7. Carefully observe the contrast between us (vv. 15-16) and God (vv. 17-19). Does this make you feel better or worse about yourself? Explain.

---

8. Praying our salvation concludes by praising the saving God. The praise is orchestrated in verses 20-22. Who are the players in this hierarchy of praises?

Who else would you like to call into the orchestra?

---

9. What does it mean for you to be saved?

What dimensions of salvation would you like to explore further?

---

10. What personal notes of praise can you add to this psalm? If you are studying this with a group, pray together now as a chamber orchestra, each contributing your own notes.

7
Praying Our Fear

Psalm 23

The world is a fearsome place. If we manage with the help of parents, teachers and friends to survive the dangers of infancy and childhood, we find ourselves launched in an adult world that is ringed with terror—accident, assault, disease, violence, conflicts. Prayer brings fear into focus and faces it. But prayer does more than bravely face fear, it affirms God's presence in it.

1. What are your recurring fears?

2. Read Psalm 23. This is a well-known psalm. It takes strenuous effort to see it in a fresh way. Is there anything here you have never noticed before?

3. There are two large metaphors in the psalm: the shepherd (vv. 1-4) and the host (vv. 5-6). Compare and contrast these two images.

4. Look carefully at the shepherd. How exactly does he care for his sheep (vv. 1-4)?

5. How does the setting of verse 4 contrast with that of verses 1-3?

6. "I fear no evil" (v. 4) is a bold statement. What does it mean for you to say that?

7. Look carefully at the host. How exactly does he provide for his guest (vv. 5-6)?

8. How many times does the first person pronoun *(I, me, my)* occur in this psalm?

What impact does this make on you?

---

9. Enemies are prominent in the psalm prayers and appear here. Who are your enemies?

---

10. What is the most comforting thing that you have experienced in the life of faith?

---

11. Psalm 23 is a weapon against fear. What fear in your life will you go to war against with this prayer as your cannon?

---

12. Pray. Name your fears and ask Christ the Shepherd and Christ the Host to relieve them.

8
Praying Our Hate

Psalm 137

W e want to be at our best before God. Prayer, we think, means presenting ourselves before God so that he will be pleased with us. We put on our "Sunday best" in our prayers. But when we pray the prayers of God's people, the Psalms, we find that will not do. We must pray who we actually are, not who we think we should be. Here is a prayer that brings out not the best but the worst in us: vile, venomous, vicious hate. Can God handle our hate?

---

1. Everyone has hated at one time or another. It is one of the basic human experiences. Be honest. Whom have you hated? Why?

---

2. Read Psalm 137. This psalm combines the loveliest lyric we can sing with the ugliest emotion we can feel. What makes verses 1-6 lovely?

What makes verses 7-9 ugly?

---

3. The Babylonian exile put God's people where they did not want to be, with no hope of returning. Have you ever been where you didn't want to be?

Do verses 1-3 express anything in your experience? Explain.

---

4. Homesickness is understandable. Sometimes it is evidence of loyalty. Sometimes it is simply irresponsibility. Remembering your own experiences, how would you evaluate verses 4-6?

---

5. Why was Israel in Babylon?

---

6. Israelites were an oft-conquered, much-trampled people. The Edomites in the past (v. 7) and the Babylonians (v. 8) in the present were oppressors. America has never been conquered. Imagine what it would be like to be the world's patsy. How might that shape your prayers?

7. Verses 7-9 are bone-chilling. This is raw hate. It is also prayer. It is easy to be honest before God with our hallelujahs; it is easy to be honest before God in our hurt; it is not easy to be honest before God in the dark emotions of our hate. How honest are you? Explain.

---

8. Jesus said "Love your enemies and pray for those who persecute you" (Mt 6:44). How can we possibly love and pray for such people?

---

9. The two dominant emotions in this prayer are self-pity (vv. 1-6) and avenging hate (vv. 7-9), neither of them particularly commendable. Praying our sins doesn't, as such, launder them. What does it do?

---

10. Most of us suppress our negative emotions (unless, neurotically, we advertise them). The way of prayer is not to cover them up so we will appear respectable, but to expose them so we can be healed. What negative emotion would you like healed?

---

11. Take any hate or dislike that you have uncovered and give it voice as you pray.

9
Praying Our Tears

Psalm 6

T ears are a biological gift of God. They are a physical means for expressing emotional and spiritual experience. But it is hard to know what to do with them. If we indulge our tears, we cultivate self-pity. If we suppress our tears, we lose touch with our feelings. But if we *pray* our tears we enter into sadnesses that integrate our sorrows with our Lord's sorrows and discover both the source of and the relief from our sadness.

---

1. When was the last time you cried—*really cried?* Explain.

---

2. Read Psalm 6. It is not popular in our culture to talk of an angry God (v. 1). What experience have you had of God's anger?

3. Compare the first verse with the last. Are the tears because of the Lord or the enemies? Explain.

---

4. "How long?" (v. 3) is a frequent question in prayer. Considering the frequency with which it is uttered in Scripture, God must welcome it. What in your life, past or present, evokes this question?

---

5. What is the cumulative effect of the three verbs *turn, deliver* and *save* in verse 4?

---

6. The emotional center of this prayer is verses 6-7. How many different ways is weeping expressed?

Why the tears? (Go through the psalm and note every possible source.)

7. Tears are often considered a sign that something is wrong with us—depression, unhappiness, frustration—and therefore either to be avoided or to be cured. But what if they are a sign of something right with us? What rightness could they be evidence of?

8. In verses 8-9 there are three phrases in parallel: *weeping, cry for mercy* and *prayer*. Are these aspects of one thing or three different things? Explain.

9. Remembering and praising (v. 5) are set forth as if they should mean something to God. Why should they?

Are you practiced and skilled in them? Explain.

10. Who do you know who is in grief? Pray for them now, using phrases from Psalm 6 to express their sorrow.

10
Praying Our Doubt
Psalm 73

Doubt is not a sin. It is an essential element in belief. Doubt is honesty. Things are not as they appear. We see contradictions between what we believe and what we experience. What is going on here? Did God give us a bum steer? Why aren't things turning out the way we were taught to expect? No mature faith avoids or denies doubt. Doubt forces faith to bedrock.

1. What doubts have you had or do you have about the Christian life?

Do you feel guilty about expressing such doubts? Why?

2. Read Psalm 73. It is full of doubt. How would you paraphrase the doubt expressed in verses 2-12?

3. Who do you know who is, as they say, "getting away with murder"?

_____

4. Self-pity is like a deadly virus. How would you express, in terms of your own life, what the psalmist says in verses 13-14?

_____

5. The key word and the pivotal center of the psalm is the word *till* in verse 17. What takes place here in the sanctuary?

_____

6. What takes place in *your* sanctuary, the place where you worship?

How do some of the psalmist's realizations and understandings come into focus in your act of worship?

_____

7. The *yet* in verse 23 links two contrasting statements. What are they?

How have you experienced this truth?

---

8. The prosperity of the wicked occupied the first part of the psalm (vv. 1-16). The presence of the Lord occupies the second (vv.17-28). What is more vivid to you, the wicked or the Lord? Explain.

---

9. The appearance of the wicked whom we envy is in utter and complete contrast to their reality (vv. 18-20). How do you discern between what you *see* (and are tempted to envy) and what *is* (and so are affirmed in obedience)?

---

10. Worship is the pivotal act in this prayer. The Christian consensus is that it is the pivotal act every week. How can worship become a more pivotal part of your experience?

---

11. In your time of prayer spend five minutes in silence, savoring God's presence, letting him restore your perspective. Then speak your praises.

11
Praying Our Death

Psalm 90

Death is not a popular subject. We live in a society characterized by the denial of death. This is unusual. Most people who have lived on this earth have given a great deal of attention to death. Preparing for a good death has been, in every century except our own, an accepted goal in life. Psalm 90 has been part of that preparation for millions of Christians.

1. When you think about your own death, what do you think about? What do you feel?

What death has affected you most deeply?

2. Read Psalm 90. Death sets a limit to our lives and stimulates reflection on the context of life, which is not death, but God. In verses 1-2, how does the psalmist set death within his view of God?

3. Review the Genesis basis of verse 3 in Genesis 2:7 and 3:17-19. How does the knowledge of your mortality affect the way you live your life?

4. Why would God be angry with you (vv.7-9)?

5. How does the psalmist describe God's anger and its effects on our lives (vv.7-11)?

6. How do you integrate this view of God with John's well-known statement "God is love"?

7. Luther commented on verse 12: "Lord, teach us all to be such arithmeticians!" What does it mean to number our days aright?

_____

8. How long do you expect to live?

How many years more does that give you?

How do you plan to live the years left to you?

_____

9. The psalmist's sense of mortality is dramatic (vv.4-6). How do modern hospitals blunt this sense of brevity and fragility?

_____

10. This prayer brings _death_ into focus. But it does far more— it brings _God_ into focus. Study the verbs in verses 14-17. What emerges as most important for you—the things that you do for the rest of your life or what God will do in your life? Explain.

11. Plato believed that philosophy was nothing more than a study of death. In the Middle Ages pastoral care concentrated on preparing you for a good death. How does your meditation on death affect the way you live your life?

12. Pray your awareness that you will die. In your prayers be conscious of Christ's death.

12
Praying
Our Praise

Psalm 150

All prayer finally, in one way or another, becomes praise. Psalm 150 is deliberately placed as the concluding prayer of the church's book of prayers. No matter how much we suffer, no matter our doubts—everything finds its way into praise, the final consummating prayer. This is not to say that other prayers are inferior to praise, only that all prayer, pursued far enough, becomes praise.

1. What circumstances or feelings in the last year have, however momentarily, made a praising person out of you?

2. Read Psalm 150. How many times is the word *praise* used in the psalm?

3. Verse 1 tells us *where* the Lord is to be praised. What is the meaning of *in his sanctuary* and *in his mighty heavens?*

4. Verse 2 tells us *why* he is to be praised. What reasons does the psalmist give?

What reasons of your own can you add?

5. Verses 3-5 tell us *how* to praise the Lord. As you read these verses, what kind of scene do you imagine?

How does this kind of worship compare with your own?

6. Verse 6 tells us *who* should praise the Lord. Do you think the "everything that has breath" is meant literally? Look hard at the exceptions. Jesus on the cross is the biggest exception—how did *that* give praise?

7. In Hebrew the first and last word of this prayer is *hallelujah* ("praise the Lord"). To what extent is your life bracketed by this word?

8. There are no short cuts to praise. If we maintain a sensitivity to all the psalms preceding this one, we will not be insensitive to all the tears and doubts and pain that are summed up into praise. What difficult circumstances in your life have found their way into praise?

9. Augustine claimed that a "Christian should be a hallelujah from head to foot." Are you? Do you want to be? What needs to be done to get you there?

10. Pray your praise. Gather the reflections and insights that have come from your study and turn them into a time of concluding and celebrative praise.

Leader's Notes

Leading a Bible discussion can be an enjoyable and rewarding experience. But it can also be *scary*—especially if you've never done it before. If this is your feeling, you're in good company. When God asked Moses to lead the Israelites out of Egypt, he replied, "O Lord, please send someone else to do it!" (Ex 4:13).

When Solomon became king of Israel, he felt the task was far beyond his abilities. "I am only a little child and do not know how to carry out my duties. . . . Who is able to govern this great people of yours?" (1 Kings 3:7, 9).

When God called Jeremiah to be a prophet, he replied, "Ah, Sovereign LORD, . . . I do not know how to speak; I am only a child" (Jer 1:6).

The list goes on. The apostles were "unschooled, ordinary men" (Acts 4:13). Timothy was young, frail and frightened. Paul's "thorn in the flesh" made him feel weak. But God's response to all of his servants—including you—is essentially the same: "My grace is sufficient for you" (2 Cor 12:9). Relax. God helped these people in spite of their weaknesses, and he can help you in spite of your feelings of inadequacy.

There is another reason why you should feel encouraged. Leading a Bible discussion is not difficult if you follow certain guidelines. You don't need to be an expert on the Bible or a trained teacher. The suggestions listed below should enable you to effectively and enjoyably fulfill your role as leader.

Preparing to Lead

1. Ask God to help you understand and apply the passage to your own life. Unless this happens, you will not be prepared to lead others. Pray too for the various members of the group. Ask God to give you an enjoyable and profitable time together studying his Word.

2. As you begin each study, read and reread the assigned Bible passage to familiarize yourself with what the author is saying. In the case of book studies, you may want to read through the entire book prior to the first study. This will give you a helpful overview of its contents.

3. This study guide is based on the New International Version of the Bible. It will help you and the group if you use this translation as the basis for your study and discussion. Encourage others to use the NIV also, but allow them the freedom to use whatever translation they prefer.

4. Carefully work through each question in the study. Spend time in meditation and reflection as you formulate your answers.

5. Write your answers in the space provided in the study guide. This will help you to express your understanding of the passage clearly.

6. It might help you to have a Bible dictionary handy. Use it to look up any unfamiliar words, names or places. (For additional help on how to study a passage, see chapter five of *Leading Bible Discussions,* IVP.)

7. Once you have finished your own study of the passage, familiarize yourself with the leader's notes for the study you are leading. These are designed to help you in several ways. First, they tell you the purpose the study guide author had in mind while writing the study. Take time to think through how the study questions work together to accomplish that purpose. Second, the notes provide you with additional background information or comments on some of the questions. This information can be useful if people have difficulty understanding or answering a question. Third, the leader's notes can alert you to potential problems you may encounter during the study.

8. If you wish to remind yourself of anything mentioned in the leader's notes, make a note to yourself below that question in the study.

Study 1. Praying Our Inattention. Psalm 1.

Purpose: To learn to prepare to pray. Much prayer flounders because there is no preparation for prayer. Our school of prayer, the Psalms, takes adequate time to prepare us to pray. Prayer is the cultivation and exploration of our best in relationship with God. It is essential not to be in a hurry. Preparation needs to be leisurely.

Question 1. Almost every study begins with an "approach" question, which is meant to be asked before the passage is read. These questions are important for several reasons.

First, they help the group to warm up to each other. No matter how well a group may know each other, there is always a stiffness that needs to be overcome before people will begin to talk openly. A good question will break the ice.

Second, approach questions get people thinking along the lines of the topic of the study. Most people will have lots of different things going on in their minds (dinner, an important meeting coming up, how to get the car fixed) that will have nothing to do with the study. A creative question will get their attention and draw them into the discussion.

Third, approach questions can reveal where our thoughts or feelings need to be transformed by Scripture. This is why it is especially important not to read the passage before the approach question is asked. The passage will tend to color the honest reactions people would otherwise give because they are of course supposed to think the way the Bible does. Giving honest responses to various issues before they find out what the Bible says may help them to see where their thoughts or attitudes need to be changed.

In this question explore some of the common experiences we have in moving from our everyday routine or preoccupation with ourselves, to attend to something special where another is more important than we are (courtship, a job interview, a special occasion).

Question 4. If the group has trouble seeing the significance of this progression, point out that the verbs go from movement to nonmovement, ending up "set in your ways."

Question 5. We prepare to pray by weaning ourselves away from listening to what everybody in family and school and culture is saying to us, and attending to what *God* is saying to us.

Question 6. Prime the pump here with some negative responses. Many people feel bored, doubtful or bewildered when reading Scripture. These feelings need to be admitted and faced. If they are not admitted and dealt with, the "delight" will be forced and become a pose.

Question 8. Some people in the group may not know what chaff is. You might briefly explain that when grain is threshed the worthless part (the seed covering and other debris) separates from the valuable grain. Later, in an ancient process known as winnowing, the grain and chaff are thrown into the air. The wind blows away the chaff because it is light, but the heavier grain falls back to earth.

Question 10. Christians have always seen prayer as one element in a two-part rhythm: God speaks to us in Scripture; we answer him in prayer. The slow, leisurely "listening-reading" of Scripture cannot be overemphasized as preparation for prayer.

Study 2. Praying Our Intimidation. Psalm 2.

Purpose: To prepare to pray by setting the world around us before the lordship of God.

Commonly we are intimidated by the world because it seems intractable to the life of faith. So we reduce our prayers to private exercises in personal virtue. We need to prepare for the practice of prayer as a world power.

Question 1. As a creative alternative to this question, bring to the group a handful of clippings from today's newspaper or this week's news magazine. Read a few. Then ask: "Do these items motivate you to pray with the same level of urgency as when you hear of a friend who has cancer or when you face a personal or family crisis? Explain why or why not."

Question 4. Meditation involves passionate attentiveness. It is not mere daydreaming on your knees. Plotting against God is common enough in the world, but is there an equivalent "plotting" in the church in consultation with God? Charles Williams says in his novel *All Hallows Eve*, that a "cruel purpose could outspeed a vague pity." Do you "plot/meditate" the world's salvation as energetically as the politicians do their strategies?

Question 5. If the discussion flounders, point out that it is possible to take the power of political evil too solemnly—to be too worried about it. A gentle mockery might be more biblical.

Question 7. The resurrection is the triumph of God over the plot of powerful Rome and Israel against God's anointed.

Question 8. It is easy and common to restrict Christ's rule to the soul. Discuss the political dimensions that are explicit in Jesus (that is, his political *purposes* for people living together in peace and justice). You will need to be ready to distinguish this from political *means* of wars and legislatures.

Question 10. Ask the members of the group to talk about one nation, other than our own, that they have a special interest in. Discuss the interest. Ask them to make a commitment, during the course of this study, to make daily intercessory prayer for that nation and its people, and to keep notes on how they feel about it.

Study 3. Praying Our Trouble. Psalm 3.
Purpose: To probe for the place of need in our lives that evokes the cry for "help" to God. To introduce the basic prayer of Psalm 3, developing familiarity with the way help is requested along with confidence in asking for it.

Question 1. We are encouraged to be self-sufficient in our society. Asking for help is widely interpreted to be a sign of weakness. As a consequence much asking for help is done on the sly or not at all. Discuss individual feeling about asking for help in this broader cultural atmosphere.

Question 2. If people in the group are unfamiliar with Absalom's conspiracy, you might wish to briefly summarize what happened in 2 Samuel 15—18. But don't spend too much time on this.

Question 3. *Deliver* has several synonyms. The most familiar is *save.* Sometimes these words are reserved exclusively for reference to the soul's eternal salvation. Push the discussion outwards, getting as much included in God's action as the imagination of the group can handle.

Question 5. It's easier to talk about threatening circumstances than people. It isn't "nice" to admit that we have enemies. If necessary, remind the group that Jesus didn't say that we weren't supposed to have them, but rather that we were supposed to pray for them. A sharp-edged sense of "enemy" is essential to prayer.

Question 10. Spend time praying for each other, and carry a list away from the meeting with each person's needs named—raw material for a week's prayer.

Study 4. Praying Our Creation. Psalm 8.

Purpose: To develop a sense of orientation as a creature of God, living in the creation of God.

The Bible pays a great deal of attention to *context,* the environment in which we live out our lives. The comprehensive name for this environment is "creation." The usual identity question of our culture is "Who am I?" It is interesting to compare it to the first question put to Adam in the garden, *"Where* are you?" God, it seems, is more interested in our geography than our psychology. And geography is an aspect of creation.

Question 1. Throughout this study encourage the group to go beyond immediately personal answers and to explore the views of our culture. What disorienting effects do our culture's idolatrous views of God and reductionist views of humanity have on us?

Question 2. Prayer keeps our attention on God, who is the comprehensive context of existence. Everything—creation and creatures—is gathered into this context and seen in the light of "your name."

Question 6. It has been common in Christian reflection on this psalm to connect *mindful* with the Incarnation.

Question 9. Environmentalists hostile to the Christian faith have often leveled the accusation that the Bible and Christians are responsible for the rapacious treatment of the land in contrast, for instance, to American Indians who have a mystical reverence for it. Explore the experiences of the group—do they feel implicated in this accusation?

Questions 11-12. We don't improve or correct our self-image by looking in the mirror or by introspective meditation, but by prayer. Encourage the use of this prayer as a means of bringing our self-image into conformity with our God-image.

Study 5. Praying Our Sin. Psalm 51.

Purpose: To realize the exact nature of what is wrong with us before God and to discover in a personal way what sin is.

Most of us carry around enormous loads of guilt that have nothing to do with God—guilt that comes from not meeting other people's expectations, or taking too seriously criticisms that have nothing to do with who we really are. This psalm helps us focus on the real issues of sin.

Question 2. Once again, if people are unfamiliar with 2 Samuel 11—12, you might briefly summarize what happened in order to provide the background for the psalm.

Question 3. You can sharpen the meaning of these sin words by developing a parallel list of synonyms that we commonly use to name what we are dissatisfied with: low self-esteem, bad self-image, hang-ups, not very smart, don't have enough money and so on. Look for ways to contrast what God thinks of us with what we think of ourselves.

Question 4. If we are always trying to make ourselves more acceptable to ourselves and others, we are in a lifelong bondage to shifting opinions and standards we can never meet. If we are open to what God will do for our sin, we enter into spacious freedom, for we are no longer in charge of making ourselves better, but letting him make us holy.

Question 5. The question intends to develop an awareness of the broken *relationship* between us and God, which remains broken even when our behavior is respectable.

Question 7. God not only forgives us, cleansing us from the guilt of sin (vv. 1-9), he renews us, creating a pure heart within us (v. 10). Christians have referred to these two aspects of salvation as *justification* and *sanctification*.

Question 11. It is almost inevitable that someone will begin making resolutions not to do "this" or "that" anymore. If they do, challenge them: the whole point of the psalm and the Christian gospel is that we can't do anything about our sin except confess it, and then submit to God's way of doing something about it.

Study 6. Praying Our Salvation. Psalm 103.

Purpose: To enter into the wealth of detail that is gathered into the act of salvation by praying Psalm 103.

When salvation is reduced by sloganeering into a password, it is banalized. Salvation is not a step-by-step procedure to go through but a vast country to explore. Prayer is the means for doing this, and Psalm 103 is an excellent guidebook.

Question 1. Encourage people to elaborate the details of whatever "best thing" is held up, but don't let the examples get separated into sacred and secular piles. Salvation is sacred, but it has the power to gather everything else into it.

Question 2. Be leisurely with this. There are no right and wrong answers.

Question 6. In your discussion of this question pay special attention to verses 11-14. The statements about heaven and earth, east and west, and a father and his children are incredibly rich in meaning.

Questions 8-9. In order to get the full impact of these verses, encourage the group to use their imagination. Try to picture the mighty angels in one section of the orchestra, the heavenly hosts (countless multitudes) in another, all other created beings and things in another, and the psalmist standing in the conductor's place. With sweeping gestures, he draws out notes of praise first from one section then another, until the entire creation—including the psalmist—is praising and worshiping the Lord. This is an overpowering scene!

If no one else mentions it, point out that each member of the orchestra is characterized by obedience. The mighty ones *do his bidding* and *obey his word* (v. 20). The heavenly hosts are *servants* who *do his will* (v. 21). Likewise, all his works are under *his dominion*. The assumption is that the psalmist and those whom the Lord has saved are also obedient to him.

Question 10. This might be the right time to have persons in the group share their own stories of salvation. As these stories are told, an alert leader can "footnote" the stories with phrases from the psalm or items from the earlier discussion.

The assumption in the study questions is that everyone in the group is "saved." That, of course, may not be so. Invite the "unsaved" to tell their stories also: What do you think of all this? How do you feel when the rest of us are talking this way?

Study 7. Praying Our Fear. Psalm 23.

Purpose: To name and then pray the fears that are in our lives.

Everybody has fears, but the culture trains us to bluff our way through them. Our psychologized age names fears "phobias" and makes them evidence of neurosis. But the world *is* a fearful place. There is much to fear, both inside us and outside us. The healthiest thing to do with fear is to name it and then pray it. Our purpose in doing this is to discover God's presence in the experience of fear.

Question 1. Some fears are based in reality, and some in fantasy. Fears based in reality serve to keep us alive a little longer; fears based in fantasy restrict the scope of our lives. Talk about the differences.

Question 2. If no one else mentions it, you might point out how many times personal pronouns (*I, me, my*) occur in the psalm. It is very personal! Did the group notice that the psalm is divided into two halves, each based on a different metaphor (see question 3)? You can encourage careful observation by naming all the metaphors, counting nouns, listing verbs, noting contrasts. But only do this if the group isn't getting anywhere on its own.

Question 5. The shepherd carried a rod (small club) for protection. His staff, which was longer and often curved at the end, was used primarily to guide and direct the sheep.

Question 6. For a sheep the "paths of righteousness" simply meant the right paths on which the shepherd guided him (although for us they have moral overtones). Therefore, when the sheep walks through the valley of the shadow of death (v. 4), it is not by accident—the shepherd has led him there and will protect him. You may have to make some distinctions here: *fearing no evil* is not the same thing as never having bad things happen to us. Prayer is not a rabbit's foot that wards off bad luck.

Question 7. The law of the desert was hospitality. If someone was running from an enemy and took refuge in a Bedouin tent, the hospitality could not be violated. That custom is implicit in the psalm. Hosts would sometimes anoint the heads of their guests with perfumed oil as a gesture of hospitality. The overflowing cup was a sign of the abundant provisions of the banquet.

Questions 9-11. Return to the discussion that came out of question 1, and review what was said. Guide the group into responsibly dealing with fears that are actually in their lives and not wandering off in conjecture about "what if."

Study 8. Praying Our Hate. Psalm 137.

Purpose: To learn first to admit and then to pray our hate.

This may be the most difficult study in the series, but it is very important. If we don't learn to do what the psalmists did, facing and speaking the very worst that is inside us, our lives of prayer will never reach bedrock.

Question 1. It is easiest to begin with childhood experiences: hating parents for punishing us or making us do something we disliked; hating the neighborhood bully; hating an awful teacher. As we become "socialized" we learn not to use that language. But the experiences and feelings continue, often unadmitted. Until we bring them to the surface, they are not available for prayer.

Question 7. Remind the group that the psalmist wants the Babylonians to experience the same atrocities they had inflicted on Israel (notice v. 8). We need to realize that parents in Israel had to watch their infants being dashed against the rocks! The horror of this does not make their hatred acceptable, but it does make it more understandable.

Question 8. If you don't have any named enemies, you can't pray for them. Recall the discussion of question 10 in the previous study (on Psalm 23). Encourage the group to make their enemy list their prayer list.

Question 9. We could, by using this prayer, end up "hating on our knees," and justifying our hate by our posture. But this psalm is embedded in a collection of prayers that trains us in confession and praise. Psalm 137 is not a stopping place; we have to go on to Psalm 138 and 139 if we are going to grow in prayer.

Study 9. Praying Our Tears. Psalm 6.

Purpose: To learn to bring emotions into the act of prayer, not sentimentally, but biologically.

The task of prayer is to bring everything we are and feel before God. Emotions are tricky. They are a *fact* of our lives, but they easily become fraudulent. Prayer keeps them honest—*if* we pray them. Sorrow is a fact of life, but difficult to distinguish from self-pity. Psalm 6 helps to make the distinction and to cultivate the sorrow.

Question 1. As this question is discussed, try to pay attention to the causes of the weeping, the source of the tears. Some weeping is manipulative, trying to get others to feel sorry for us. Some weeping is selfish, from not getting our own way. Some weeping is compassionate, a deep feeling for the suffering in others. Don't be critical of anything that is expressed, but keep it in mind for later development.

Questions 2-3. In question 2 ask the group to search the psalm for every possible source of David's tears. Explore why David would assume that the difficulties in his life—at least in part—were a result of the Lord's anger.

Question 7. There have been times in the history of faith when tears have been evidence of a deep life in Christ, feeling his agony on the cross and his weeping over Jerusalem, and participating in it. Our culture emphasizes the opposite: the happy Christian and the have-it-altogether saint. Are we missing something? Probe the discussion for signs of healthy tears: tears that arise from loss (bereavement, separation), tears that arise from repentance (something wrong with me) or compassion (something wrong in others). All other tears are probably either immature (childish) or wrong (sinful).

Study 10. Praying Our Doubt. Psalm 73.

Purpose: To bring doubt into the act of prayer by reflecting on Psalm 73.

It is always a mistake to deny doubt or suppress it. But what else is there to do with it? It can't be ignored, for it unnerves and unsettles us. The biblical way is to *pray* doubt, and Psalm 73 shows us how.

Question 1. One way to deal with doubts is to charge them head on with a cannonade of arguments. Such assaults are sometimes helpful, but many people are merely intimidated and decide to keep their doubts quietly to themselves. If voicing a doubt makes us liable to attack, we are going to be cautious about speaking up. So you might have to provide some reassurance here to encourage discussion.

Questions 3. Doubt arises when there is a discrepancy between what we think should happen if God is in charge, and what in fact we see happening. Get as much illustrative material from the group as you can decently manage.

Question 6. Worship is not argument. It is attending to the invisible because we believe that the quiet God we can't see is more solid and dynamic than the noisily arrogant people we can see. The practice of worship doesn't explain evil; it puts it in perspective. And it doesn't cure doubt, but uses it as fuel to pray more ardently.

Questions 10-11. It is important to lead the discussion in such a way that worship is understood as what we *do,* not what we *feel.* Worship is an orienting act in which we decide to let our lives be shaped by God instead of doing the best we can against whatever makes life difficult for us. It develops habitual faith (with doubts nagging at the edges) in contrast to habitual doubt (with faith nagging at the edges).

Study 11. Praying Our Death. Psalm 90.

Purpose: To come to grips with our mortality by facing the fact that we are going to die—maybe sooner, maybe later than we think—and to do so by praying Psalm 90.

There is no particular virtue in simply thinking about death. It can be neurotic morbidity. But there is a Christian way to face death that sharply defines and sanely develops our dependence on and trust in God.

Question 1. What is said and felt at funerals sometimes reveals our attitudes to death. If the group needs additional prompting with this question, ask follow-up questions such as: How do you feel at a funeral? What do you say to people who are bereaved? What has been your experience with the dying? Do you avoid them? Are you overly cheery?

Question 2. At the end of our lives, there is God. Death forces us, rather dramatically, to remember God. Some medieval monks slept in their coffins every night to keep themselves aware of the limits to their strength and the limitlessness of God's mercy. Does that appeal to you?

Questions 5-6. The biblical writers don't hesitate to use human words to describe the nature and action of God. This lack of caution is a great boon; there is nothing bloodless or abstract in the biblical God. But it also sets a difficult task for our imaginations. We must discriminate carefully what is meant, or we will end up with a picture of God which is only our own self enlarged. The "anger" of God requires interpretation. In one sense, God is not angry the way we are angry—flying off the handle because he is frustrated. But in another sense, our experience of anger tells something profound about God. Explore what it is.

Question 11. The crucifixion death of Jesus is obviously the best example of preparing for a good death. Christians learn how to die by observing how Jesus died and by participating in it. The pattern set for us is not stoical but redemptive.

Study 12. Praying Our Praise. Psalm 150.

Purpose: To realize the comprehensiveness of praise and to set as a personal goal that all our prayers will eventually end up in praise.

Prayer almost never begins in praise (it usually begins in hurt), but if pursued long enough, it will finally develop into praise. This doesn't mean that every prayer we make is capped off with praise, but that the life of prayer itself is always reaching toward praise. Most of the prayers in the Psalter, our training book in prayer, are not praises but laments. But they all end up at Psalm 150, praising the Lord. If we persist in prayer, we also will end up at Psalm 150, praising.

Question 2. The Psalter is arranged into five books: 1—41, 42—72, 73—89, 90—106, 107—150. As preparation for this study, turn to the last psalm in each of the books and note its concluding verse. This "sense of an ending" gathers momentum through the Psalter.

Psalm 150 is not, by itself, the conclusion of the Psalms. There are five "hallelujah" psalms, one for each book of the Psalter. These gather all the prayers offered in Israel and the church into praise. In order to see Psalm 150 in context, you may wish to observe a few of the complementary emphases in these five psalms (146—150).

Question 3. This study is organized around the following outline: *where* to praise the Lord (v. 1), *why* to praise him (v. 2), *how* to praise him (vv. 3-5) and *who* should praise him (v. 6). Various questions in the study point out this outline. However, if your group is more advanced you may wish to begin question 3 by asking: "What brief outline would you give to this psalm?" or "How would you divide this psalm into sections, and what brief title would you give to each one?"

The phrase *in his sanctuary* has been understood in various ways. Some commentators believe it is synonymous with *in his mighty heavens.* If so, then it refers to God's dwelling place. Others believe it is a reference to the temple, God's earthly sanctuary, in contrast to *in his mighty heavens,* his heavenly sanctuary. If so, then the psalmist is calling both earthly and heavenly worshipers to praise the Lord. If the group has difficulty answering this question, you might mention these possibilities and ask which one they feel best fits the context of the psalm.

Question 5. Encourage the group to imagine they are present at this worship service. What would they see and hear? What mood would fill the air? Then encourage them to compare this with their own corporate worship experience. What elements of worship in this psalm would they like to incorporate into their own worship?

Question 7. Guard against glibness here. It is easy to talk about what we "should" do in praising God and being grateful for what we have and are. But it is a lifelong assignment, not a weekend job.

Question 8. If you have time, you may wish to briefly review the different kinds of prayer that have been studied so far. Take the experience of each psalm (except 1 and 2) and discuss how those experiences can eventually become praise (or maybe already have in some people in the group). But don't rush it. It may take many years before some of these prayers "arrive" at Psalm 150.

Eugene H. Peterson is pastor of Christ Our King Presbyterian Church in Bel Air, Maryland, and adjunct professor at St. Mary's Seminary in Baltimore. He is also the author of A Long Obedience in the Same Direction, Traveling Light, Run with the Horses *and* Earth and Altar.